BRONTOSAURUS
THE THUNDER LIZARD

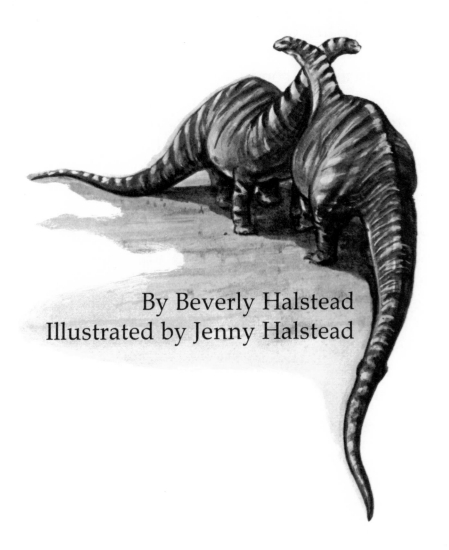

By Beverly Halstead
Illustrated by Jenny Halstead

GOLDEN PRESS • NEW YORK
Western Publishing Company, Inc., Racine, Wisconsin

Introduction

The dinosaur on which this story is based lived some 150 million years ago, during the Upper Jurassic period. It was discovered in the rocks of the Morrison Formation in Utah, but many other similar dinosaurs have been found in Colorado and in Europe. The first scientific description was written in 1877 by O. C. Marsh of Yale University. He based the description on an almost complete skeleton, and he named the dinosaur *Apatosaurus ajax.* This type of dinosaur is popularly known as *Brontosaurus,* or Thunder Lizard.

It is thought that *Apatosaurus ajax* weighed only about six and a half pounds at birth, the weight of a newborn human baby, but that it grew to an enormous thirty-three tons and a length of seventy-two feet. Sections of the leg bones show annual growth rings, and up to 120 rings have been counted.

Footprints show that *Apatosaurus* had a big pad on each foot to take its great weight. It also had one claw and four small hoofs on each of its front feet, and three claws and two hoofs on each of its back feet. The claws probably helped it grip soft ground. Footprints also show the ripping claws of flesh-eating dinosaurs that almost certainly attacked young brontosaurs.

This book tells the story of one brontosaur, *Apatosaurus ajax,* whom we have called Ajax.

The warm sand surrounded the eggs, which were nearly ready to hatch. First there were faint taps, then several shells began to crack. Baby brontosaurs poked their heads out into the glaring sunlight. They rolled over, out of their eggs and onto the sand. Their first instinct was to find shade. Suddenly they were overshadowed by dark shapes, and leathery-winged pterosaurs with fearsome beaks swooped down to feast on the newly hatched dinosaurs. A few of the babies escaped the onslaught by stumbling to the safety of the dark undergrowth.

Nests have been found containing 15 to 20 brontosaur eggs each, with each egg about 8 inches in diameter. This seems small compared with the size of adult brontosaurs. However, a larger egg would have required a thicker shell, which would not have allowed oxygen to pass through—so the developing embryo would have been unable to breathe.

Just as baby crocodiles are easy prey for marabou storks, so baby dinosaurs would have been easy prey for pterosaurs.

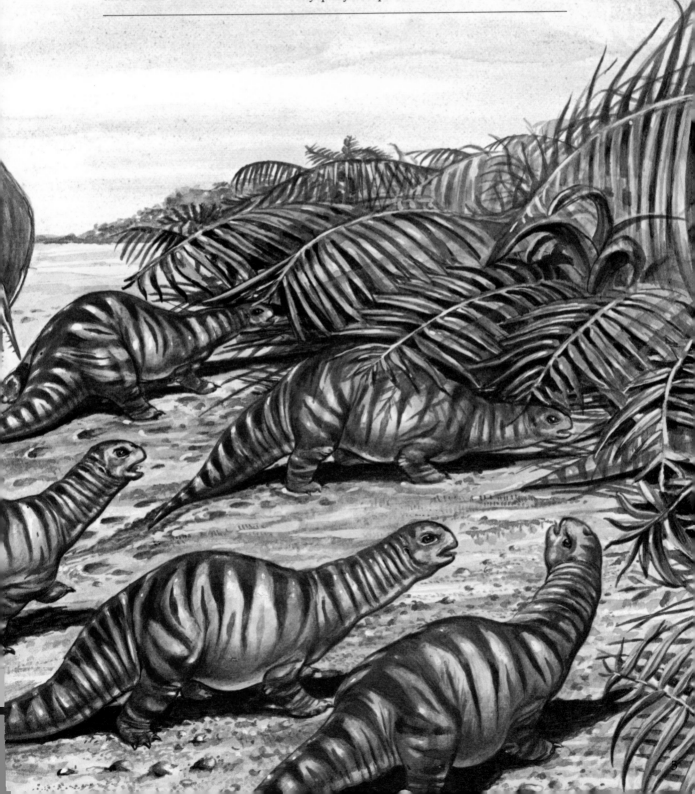

Two of the young dinosaurs who fled into the undergrowth stayed close to each other. They ate small insects and soft juicy leaves. Bright green lizards flashed past them. Occasionally *Archaeopteryx*, a bird with a long tail, glided down and chased the dinosaurs along the ground. Sometimes *Archaeopteryx* climbed tree trunks, using the three claws on the front of its wings.

At night, when the dinosaurs were sleeping, small, furry, shrewlike mammals came out of the undergrowth to hunt for beetles and worms.

We know what else lived at the same time as the brontosaurs through fossil remains found buried in the rocks, and we can tell the age of the rocks by radioactivity. The other creatures found include other dinosaurs; the flying pterosaurs, *Archaeopteryx*; lizards; small mammals; owls; and beetles and centipedes. Among the ferns were the first true flowering plants, such as *Magnolia*.

One day, when the young brontosaurs were browsing in a glade in the forest, they were surprised by three long-legged meat-eating dinosaurs, *Coelurus*. The carnivores pounced on

the nearer of the brontosaurs, tearing him open with their strong claws and devouring him. The surviving brontosaur, Ajax, escaped into the undergrowth as fast as he could.

Ajax wandered on and on, intent on only one thing—finding food. For he was growing bigger all the time. His dusty skin began to peel, uncovering a brighter, shiny one. His neck became longer, making it easier for him to reach higher for young leaves. However, he still sometimes had to eat older, tougher plants, which were difficult to digest. One day he came to a dried-up riverbed. Here he found many rounded pebbles, which he picked up in his mouth and swallowed. In this way Ajax acquired his first set of stomach stones. Now when he had to eat tough, fibrous plants, the stones in his stomach pounded the fibers and made them easier to digest.

While Ajax was busily collecting the pebbles, a small herd of *Hypsilophodon* entered the clearing. Soon they were all around him, grazing contentedly on the plants. Ajax looked up with a start, and he lashed his tail as a warning in case they were flesh-eaters who would attack him. But they merely bounded away into the forest.

We cannot be sure about the brontosaur's coloring, as it has not been preserved. It is reasonable to assume, though, that very young brontosaurs were patterned for protective camouflage, and that their skin gradually faded as they grew and turned gray as they aged.

We can be certain the brontosaur was a plant-eater from its teeth, and from plant remains that have been preserved in some brontosaurs' stomachs. Fossils have revealed highly polished stones in the stomach region. Their function is believed to have been the same as that of the stomach stones found in crocodiles.

Ajax roamed through the forest, eating and growing.
Years passed. One year during the rainy season there was
a tremendous storm. The wind tore through the forest,
bringing tall trees crashing to the ground. Everything
swayed, and branches flew through the air. A jagged
streak of lightning lit the sky, followed immediately by a
resounding crack of thunder. Then the skies opened and
torrents of rain poured down.

Ajax ran to escape the torrential downpour, the crashing
trees, the lightning and the cracking thunder. He ran and
ran, not knowing where he was going, until eventually the
storm subsided and he fell down, exhausted, to sleep.

When Ajax woke he was no longer in the forest he had known all his life. There were fewer trees and less shade. He ambled along, feeding as he went. At last he reached the edge of the forest. There before him was an open plain. Grazing in the distance was a herd of dinosaurs, *Camptosaurus*.

For some time Ajax stayed near the edge of the forest. Then, cautiously, he ventured farther and farther out across the plain. Ahead, the plants were a deeper green, which he knew meant lush, tender food.

From fossilized wood and plant remains, and from dinosaur footprints, we know what the landscape was like: forests, plains, and muddy swamps.

Ajax moved slowly across the vast plain and found himself in a swamp at the edge of a lake. He waded into the water and began pulling up plants and scooping up mouthfuls of water weeds. On nearby sandbanks small groups of squat, heavily armored *Acanthopholis* peacefully chewed horsetails. Blue dragonflies hovered over the water or clung to the weeds. This was an ideal place.

Suddenly Ajax saw what looked like two scaly logs moving fast toward him. Their speed increased as they closed in. Their

huge mouths opened. Ajax quickly lifted his head out of the water, turned around, and lashed his tail. The two crocodiles moved off after smaller and easier prey.

Because of Ajax's great size, his skin would have become very hot during the day. He would, therefore, have wanted to spend many hours wallowing in water to keep cool. The nostril on the top of the head is a sign of an air breather that spends a lot of time in water.

Some time later, as Ajax was wandering over a sandy hillside, he heard a piercing scream. He hurried toward the sound and saw a dinosaur like himself being attacked by a fierce flesh-eater, *Ceratosaurus*. Ajax rushed at the attacker, lashing his tail. The suddenness of his onslaught made the *Ceratosaurus* pause, and Ajax crashed his tail across its back. The *Ceratosaurus* turned and fled, leaving the two brontosaurs standing side by side. Only then did Ajax feel the sharp pain in his tail. It was broken.

Now Ajax had a companion, a young female brontosaur. If they stayed together they would be safer from attacks by flesh-eaters. Ajax's tail gradually healed, but he always had a thick, bony lump where the broken bones had grown back together.

Of the many brontosaur skeletons excavated, one had a large bony lump in its tail, showing that the tail had been fractured during life. This specimen can be seen in the University Museum, Kansas.

Ajax and his companion spent their days feeding and wading in the swamp. Eventually they reached the open lakes, where they met other brontosaurs. As they waded deeper into the water they found that they were able to swim, pawing the bottom with their front feet. With their bodies under water they could breathe easily by poking their heads just above the surface.

Evidence that these dinosaurs could swim comes from fossil footprints in the Paluxy River, Texas. Trackways at the river bottom show only front footprints. (There is an occasional back footprint where the dinosaur put the back foot down to turn and swim in another direction.) Since the dinosaurs could not have been walking on their front legs only, they must have been swimming.

Months passed, and Ajax and his companion stayed together. One day as they were feeding on the shores of the lake they saw a herd of dinosaurs like themselves moving through the trees at the edge of the forest. The two young dinosaurs walked across the flat marshy ground toward the forest. As they trampled the shrubs underfoot, clouds of insects rose. A flock of pterosaurs swooped down, snapping up the insects in their strong beaks.

When Ajax and his companion reached the herd, the large, lumbering adults allowed the two to join them. They all moved off together, the younger ones protected by the adults.

Sometimes, when Ajax moved toward the head of the herd, one of the older males would hit him with his tail to make sure he kept his place.

Eventually the herd reached a large inlet where a series of streams entered a lake. Here the dinosaurs settled down and remained for many years. Here, too, Ajax grew to a mature adult.

Footprints show that brontosaurs lived in herds, and that when they were on the move the younger adults walked between the very large mature adults. There is no evidence of very young brontosaurs in these herds, so it is safe to assume that they did not join a herd until they were nearly adults.

When Ajax was fully grown he several times challenged the leader of the herd. Each time he was firmly struck across the neck by the leader's tail and was forced to retreat.

One day, though, Ajax stood his ground. As if responding to a signal, the rest of the herd drew back, leaving Ajax and the leader alone. The two dinosaurs stood side by side, head to tail, and this was the way they fought. Each lashed his tail with all his strength at the other's neck. Ajax had the

advantage: he was younger and stronger, and the bony lump in his tail gave him added force. At last the leader weakened, dropped his neck, and backed away, defeated. Ajax was the new leader of the herd.

The assumption that brontosaurs fought for leadership is based on observations of the activities of tropical reptiles in their native habitat.

Together Ajax and his companion led the herd. They spent most of the year around the creeks of the lake, but every spring they moved to the forest to feed on the new shoots. And every spring, in a shady patch of ground at the edge of the forest, Ajax's mate and the other females in the herd laid their eggs. They covered them with dead leaves and dry ferns

and scraped a mound of sand over the nest. Then they left the eggs to hatch on their own.

Many fossilized broken eggshells have been found by themselves. Occasionally an adult skeleton has been found close by.

After the herd had lived in and around the lake for several years, the water in the creeks began to dry up. The brontosaurs could no longer wallow in the shallow water, and there was not enough food. The herd had to move on.

Ajax, his mate, and the stronger dinosaurs led the herd along dried-up riverbeds until they came to a vast desert. Far in the distance were cloud-covered hills. If they were to find water, the dinosaurs had to cross the desert and reach the hilly area.

Under a blazing sun, they set off. It was a cruel journey. With no food and no water, the older and weaker dinosaurs collapsed on the sand and were left to die. By the time the herd reached the hills, it had lost half its members.

Fossilized remains of many early brontosaurs have been found in western Europe in what was a 75-mile-wide desert separating a hilly region from an inland sea or large lake. The brontosaurs' death is presumed to have been caused by the conditions described here.

As they neared the hills, the dinosaurs found lakes and rivers, swamps and lush vegetation. Instead of keeping together the herd spread out, all hurrying to the shore for water and food. Suddenly a pack of giant *Allosaurus* appeared from the rocky ground. They surrounded the scattered, tired brontosaurs and tore them to pieces. The remaining brontosaurs quickly formed a circle around the females and younger ones, but the flesh-eaters launched themselves on them, slashing and ripping the flanks of the herd with the daggerlike talons of their hind legs.

The brontosaurs lashed their tails at the attackers, who eventually retreated and contented themselves with gorging on the bodies of the brontosaurs they had already killed. At last the danger passed, and Ajax led the few survivors to the safety of the lake. Many had been killed in the battle, including Ajax's companion and mate.

Gradually, as the years passed, the herd recovered its strength. Younger, more powerful brontosaurs grew up, and Ajax's leadership was challenged more and more often. The day came when a young male stood his ground, despite severe blows from Ajax's tail. At last Ajax had no more energy for the fight. He lowered his head, turned, and walked away from the herd forever.

Ajax was 120 years old. He lay down in the warm sand. Nearby a nest of brontosaur eggs began to hatch. Hungry pterosaurs swooped down, but a sudden movement from Ajax's tail alarmed them, and the hatchlings scuttled to safety. Ajax closed his eyes for the last time. All was still.